Britain and European Integration

Blackwell
Publishing

Britain and European Integration
Views from Within

edited by Anand Menon

Blackwell Publishing
In association with *The Political Quarterly*

Published by Blackwell Publishing
9600 Garsington Road, Oxford OX4 2DK, UK
350 Main Street, Malden, MA 02148-5018, USA
550 Swanston Street, Carlton South, Melbourne, Victoria 3053, Australia

First published in *The Political Quarterly*, vol. 75, no. 3, 2004
by Blackwell Publishing Ltd

Library of Congress Cataloging-in-Publication Data has been Applied for

A catalogue record for this title is available from the British Library

ISBN 1-4051-2672-8 (paperback)

The publisher's policy is to use permanent paper from mills that operate a sustainable forestry policy,
and which has been manufactured from pulp processed using acid-free and elementary chlorine-free
practices. Furthermore, the publisher ensures that the text paper and cover board
used have met acceptable environmental accreditation standards.

For further information on
Blackwell Publishing, visit our website:
http://www.blackwellpublishing.com

Contents

The European Research Institute and   vi
The Political Quarterly

Introduction   1
ANAND MENON

1973–1975   7
MICHAEL PALLISER

1975–1979   11
DONALD MAITLAND

1979–1985   15
MICHAEL BUTLER

1985–1990   19
DAVID HANNAY

1990–1995   23
JOHN KERR

1995–2000   27
STEPHEN WALL

2000–2003   31
NIGEL SHEINWALD

2003–   35
JOHN GRANT

Conclusion   39
ANAND MENON

Notes   47

The Contributors   49

The European Research Institute
and *The Political Quarterly*

The European Research Institute (ERI) is one of the largest academic institutions devoted to the study of Europe in the world. Launched in 2001 by Prime Minister Tony Blair, it was funded by a generous grant of some £4.5 million from the government's Joint Infrastructure Fund.

The Institute is home to some two hundred graduate students studying for a variety of masters and doctoral courses. Its academic staff represent a unique concentration of expertise on all aspects of contemporary Europe. In addition, and as a function of its standing as a national centre of excellence, the ERI is committed to fostering public debate and understanding on issues related to Europe.

During its first two years it has hosted events attended by speakers including Foreign Secretary Jack Straw, Defence Minister Geoff Hoon, and numerous ambassadors and European Commissioners. For further information about the ERI, contact its Director, Anand Menon, on a.menon@bham.ac.uk

The Political Quarterly was founded in 1930 by Leonard Woolf, Kingsley Martin and William Robson, and ever since has consistently explored and promoted debate about the key issues of the day. The journal is dedicated to political and social reform and has long acted as a conduit between policy-makers, commentators and academics. *The Political Quarterly* has a tradition of accepting serious and thought-provoking articles on current issues written in plain, jargon-free English.

Introduction

ANAND MENON

This volume originated in an event co-hosted at the Institute of Directors on 9 January 2004 by Birmingham University's European Research Institute and S. J. Berwin, one of Britain's leading law firms. The occasion was a unique round table discussion between the eight Permanent Representatives to the European Community (EC) or, since 1993, the European Union (EU) who, in turn, have represented the United Kingdom following its accession in 1973. The round table provided an unprecedented opportunity to glean a 'view from within' about not only the role of the Permanent Representative in both the UK administrative system and the European Union, but also about Britain's evolving relationship with European integration.

The contributions to this collection represent reworked versions of the eight-minute presentations made by the Permanent Representatives at the round table. Each of the contributors was asked to address a series of questions relating to:

- their own experience of EU matters prior to being posted to Brussels;
- the place of the Permanent Representative in the wider British adminis-trative system;
- their experiences of working in Brussels;
- their reflections on the changes that have occurred in the workings of the EC/EU; and
- their impressions of the nature of the broader relationship between the United Kingdom and the European Union.

Permanent Representatives are key figures in both national and EU systems. A recent study of the Committee of Permanent Representatives identifies five functions they perform: intermediaries between the national government and the EU institutions; participants in the preparation and coordination of national positions; participants in the activities and decision making of EU institutions; participants in intergovernmental cooperation between the member states; and participants in decision making within the framework of the Union's external relations.[1] The post involves a huge workload,[2] and the Permanent Representatives are, in a sense, never 'off-duty', having to defend national interests on informal as well as formal occasions.[3] For our purposes, the position they occupy in the EU and national systems provides them with a uniquely informed perspective on both, and on the interactions between them.

© The Political Quarterly Publishing Co. Ltd. 2004
Published by Blackwell Publishing Ltd, 9600 Garsington Road, Oxford OX4 2DQ, UK and 350 Main Street, Malden, MA 02148, USA

Britain's representatives

The first cluster of questions relate to the role of the Permanent Representative within the British administrative system, beginning with the nature of the posting itself. What kind of person is appointed as Permanent Representative? What prior expertise in, and experience of, handling EU-related affairs did the various individuals possess before taking up the post in Brussels? The answers to such questions would provide insights into both where the post of Permanent Representative lies in the career structure of the Foreign and Commonwealth Office, and the extent to which Britain—and the FCO in particular (all of the Ambassadors having been professional diplomats)—has developed a cadre of EU specialists groomed not only to take up the post, but also to fill the other key administrative positions relating to Britain's relationship with the EC/EU.

Second, the contributors were asked to reflect upon the functions carried out by the Permanent Representative. Is the post a diplomatic assignment like any other? Or, rather, is it one requiring far greater detailed and specific sectoral expertise than 'normal' ambassadorial positions? If so, is it appropriate that the post of Permanent Representative still be held by a career diplomat? Whatever the answers to these questions, they will shed an interesting light on the changing nature of diplomacy in an age when foreign and domestic policy are increasingly difficult to separate, particularly in the context of EU membership.

More broadly, each of the contributors was asked to reflect upon the role and functions of the Permanent Representative within the system in place in the United Kingdom for the coordination of its EU policies. There is little need to rehearse in detail here the often complex issue of coordination.[4] Yet it is worth noting the specific incentives and problems confronting those who attempt it in the context of EU policy. In terms of incentives, the importance of securing favourable outcomes in Brussels has never been greater. The EU has become an authoritative decision making arena across an increasing range of policy fronts, and governments are under close scrutiny from their publics and press to ensure that national concerns are effectively represented and defended in Brussels. Efficient coordination may well enhance the ability of a member state to secure its policy objectives in EU negotiations via a coherent presentation and defence of them. As for obstacles confronting would-be coordinators, these include the institutional fragmentation of the EU, its instability, the openness of the EU policy agenda, and the sheer range of interests and actors affected by its activities and engaged, either directly or indirectly, in its policy processes.

Despite these obstacles, however, the academic literature has tended to emphasise the effectiveness of the British coordination system relative to those in place in other member states. Scholarly studies have largely argued that an effective coordination machine, centred on the European Secretariat of the Cabinet Office, working in the context of a Whitehall system that remains apolitical, that is based on norms of trust, openness and information sharing,

2

and that—until devolution at least—benefited from the administrative centralisation of the British state, has performed very well in terms of its ability to coordinate policy towards Brussels.[5] More specific studies have highlighted the effectiveness of the role played by the UK's Permanent Representation to the EU (UKRep) in the coordination process.[6]

European integration

Moving beyond the confines of Britain, the contributors were also asked to reflect on their experience of working in Brussels. Permanent Representatives are uniquely placed to assess the effectiveness and 'style' of one of the most powerful and important, though elusive, EU bodies, namely the Committee of Permanent Representatives (COREPER).[7] Created at the time of the inception of the European Economic Community, COREPER II is a standing committee composed of the Permanent Representatives of the member states.[8] It is widely recognised as 'one of the most powerful organs within the EU's institutional structure',[9] and plays a key role within the Council apparatus and in the Union more broadly.[10] Its location within the EU institutional system provides it with a unique vantage point. Vertically, it is situated between the expert working groups that first negotiate proposed legislation and the ministers themselves—the 'collective bottle-neck through which the work of the Council flows'.[11] No formal voting takes place in COREPER—ministers sitting in the Council of Ministers alone have the right to vote—but, on legislative matters, it is estimated that some 90 per cent of legislation is effectively agreed upon before reaching the ministers themselves. Horizontally, because of the range of issues they deal with, the Permanent Representatives are ideally placed to work across a range of different policy sectors to prepare agenda items for the vast array of Council formations.

As Kassim points out, COREPER's location both at the intersection between various Council formations and where the political meets the technical, and its function as the filter through which virtually all items of Union business must pass, make it a crucial venue for promoting and defending national interests. Consequently, 'within national capitals, the point at which issues appear on COREPER's agenda is a crucial one, and often the moment at which formal inter-departmental coordination processes are initiated'.[12]

Moreover, because COREPER performs the dual function of acting both as a 'bridge to national capitals' and 'a clearing house for the Council',[13] it has generated debates in the academic literature concerning its *modus operandi*. Jeffery Lewis has contrasted the 'intergovernmentalist' and 'sociological' images of the institution. Whilst the former is based on an 'individual, strategic rationality and the asymmetrical advantages of relative power',[14] the latter, to which he subscribes, presents a far different picture. Lewis emphasises five predominant features of the COREPER decision making style: 'diffuse reciprocity, thick trust, mutual responsiveness, a consensus-reflex, and a culture of compromise'.[15] The insights of eight individuals with personal experience of the committee and its workings should certainly provide useful empirical evidence one way or the other.

COREPER, of course, represents only a small part of the overall institutional system of the Union. Consequently, the contributors were also asked to reflect upon the functioning of the EC/EU system more generally, in the hope that their insights would generate a picture of the changes that have occurred to it over time. Again, the academic literature has generated many claims and counterclaims on this subject. For intergovernmentalists, the member states are supreme, controlling European integration via periodic Intergovernmental Conferences, and through their ultimate control of decision making in the Council. For others, variously labelled neofunctionalists or supranationalists, the history of European integration has been one of gradual yet steady accretion of power by the supranational institutions at the expense of the member states.

The contributors were not asked to venture explicitly into the jargon-ridden minefield of the academic debates about European integration. Yet they were requested to address certain questions regarding the nature of the EC/EU system, the answers to which would doubtless shed some light on academic quarrels:

- To what extent has the Permanent Representative's role been wider than simply negotiation within COREPER?
- How intensively have contacts been sought with the other major institutions—notably the Commission and the European Parliament (EP)?
- How important are these institutions to the effective functioning of the Union?
- What have been the effects of successive rounds of enlargement?
- How has the appearance of new issues on the EU's agenda (ranging from the single market, to the euro, to justice and home affairs, to the European Security and Defence Policy) affected the functioning of the Union?

The 'awkward partner'?

Finally, and by way of bringing these various strands together, the contributors considered the nature of the UK's relationship with the EU. In contrast to the overwhelmingly positive assessments of the role of the British administration in its dealings with Brussels, examinations of the political relationship have been far more critical, stressing Britain's status as an 'awkward partner',[16] and the numerous opportunities that have been squandered to rectify this situation and ensure enhanced British influence over the process of European integration.[17] Certainly, relations between the UK and the EU have been fraught on many occasions since the former's accession in 1973. The contributors were asked to provide their assessment of the changing nature of this relationship and in particular to reflect upon the impact of both an increasingly aggressive press and often febrile political atmosphere on Britain's relationship with the EC/EU.

4

It has proved to be quite a challenge to transform the proceedings of a round table held in January into an edited collection fit for publication in July. I would like to express my heartfelt thanks to all those who contributed to making this possible. First, to Caroline Bowman, at the time Secretary of the European Research Institute, without whom the original round table would never have been organised in the first place. Also to S. J. Berwin, in part for generously agreeing to finance the original event, but also for the tireless efforts of their staff in making it the success it was. Thanks are also due both to the editors of *The Political Quarterly* and to Blackwell's for their efficiency in considering and turning round the manuscript so quickly. As ever, Hussein Kassim was generous with his time, and perceptive in his comments, which have made the introduction and conclusion far better than they otherwise would have been. Andy Charlton and Colm O'Callaghan made characteristically invaluable contributions to the event. Most importantly, I would also like to record my gratitude to the eight ambassadors who, quite apart from agreeing to participate in the original round table, subsequently exposed themselves to my hectoring, chivvying and nitpicking with efficiency and good humour. I hope that they will consider this collection an adequate recompense for their efforts. Finally, it should be emphasised that the opinions expressed in the introduction and conclusion are, except where explicitly indicated otherwise, those of myself as the editor of this collection and are not necessarily shared by any of the contributors.

1973–1975

MICHAEL PALLISER

My exposure to the relationship between the UK and the EEC began early: partly when I was Prime Minister Harold Wilson's Private Secretary responsible for foreign affairs, from spring 1966 to summer 1969; but particularly when, in the autumn of 1969, I went to the British Embassy in Paris as number two to Christopher Soames, the Conservative politician and former minister. He had been appointed Ambassador—with considerable astuteness—by Prime Minister Wilson and Foreign Secretary George Brown in the hope that this well known pro-European son-in-law of Winston Churchill would somehow or other convince General de Gaulle that the UK ought to be allowed to join the EEC. This was beginning to seem far from likely when French domestic politics—unpredictable as ever—reared its head. A few nights before taking up my new post, I heard on the midnight news of General de Gaulle's enforced retirement, and realised that this would make my life in Paris much easier. Indeed, I was fortunate enough to be present as interpreter at the meeting between Prime Minister Heath and President Pompidou at the Elysée Palace in May 1971, which ended after a couple of days with their declaring to a fairly startled world and a very startled press that they believed that Britain should join the European Community.

Not long after the Heath–Pompidou meeting I was appointed Ambassador to the EC in Brussels. The negotiations for Britain's entry were still in full swing, though already nearing a conclusion. It was a fascinating period. My team in Brussels was a kind of support group for the negotiations, consisting mainly of young men and women from the relevant Whitehall departments concerned with our possible membership—and including from the Foreign Office a certain young David Hannay!

The negotiating team itself, which I then joined in Brussels, came over from London for each negotiating session. It was led by Sir Con O'Neill under the ministerial guidance of Geoffrey Rippon, the government's chief negotiator. My task was essentially to ensure that the London team had all the support and assistance it needed from my people in Brussels and to provide the negotiators with such extra information and judgements as I was able to contribute as the result of my permanent presence on the ground in the city where the negotiations were taking place.

The general atmosphere of the negotiations throughout the summer and into the autumn was broadly positive. There were, however, still several difficult issues that could potentially have scuppered a deal. Over the weeks, these were gradually resolved. Yet one in particular proved very difficult. This was the Common Fisheries Policy (CFP), cooked up at the last moment by the Six and presented to us and the other candidate countries more or less on a 'take it or leave it' basis. As far as Norway was concerned, it was largely this issue that resulted in Oslo's rejection of membership. For our part, the CFP also presented us with not inconsiderable problems. I remember sitting up late into the night in one of those dreadful rooms in the Council building in Brussels with Geoffrey Rippon, a large map of the United Kingdom spread out in front of us. He traced the coast of the UK from Conservative seat to Conservative seat, trying to work out how many Conservative MPs might be at risk if we adopted this policy. The answer was reasonably satisfactory, so in the end, and after some negotiated change, we accepted the policy. I am, of course, oversimplifying grossly; but that evening illustrated neatly the extent of the interplay between domestic politics and our involvement with European integration.

The following year, after the completion of the negotiations, was a transitional one. But I was to all intents and purposes already a Permanent Representative. I attended meetings of COREPER, British Ministers came to Council meetings and, although it was not until 1 January 1973 that I formally became Permanent Representative, I had had a year of getting used to the post.

The Office of the UK Representative (as my outfit was called) was quite unlike any normal British Embassy. For a start, well over a third of the staff, especially the more senior ones, came not from the Diplomatic Service but from the Home Civil Service. I was fortunate in that the Prime Minister had instructed that our office in Brussels was to be of high calibre, and consequently I had some exceptionally able people working with me. My second in command was Bob Goldsmith, an outstanding man from the DTI. Next came Jon Dixon, equally good, from the Ministry of Agriculture and a talented musician to boot. My senior counsellor from the Foreign Office was Ewen Fergusson, later to be our ambassador in Paris. And so it went on. I wish there was time to mention them all. Suffice it to say that both the Treasury men in the team subsequently became Permanent Secretaries in Whitehall, as did others from Home departments; and most of the Foreign Office people became ambassadors in due course. Several others transferred after their time in UKRep to either the Commission or the Council Secretariat, where they made excellent contributions. It was both an unusual and an exceptionally talented team, very hard working and very loyal. To manage it was made easier by the quality of the people.

From time to time, there could be difficulties, usually arising from disagreements between departments in London and the contradictory instructions they sent to 'their men' in Brussels. But I was in any case visiting London every Friday to attend the coordinating meeting in the Cabinet Office, at which policy towards the EEC was defined. It was not therefore too difficult to iron out any difficulties by personal contact with the senior people concerned. I had to work harder in Brussels than almost anywhere else; but it was immensely rewarding.

So too was my relationship with my colleagues from the other member states in COREPER. The eight other ambassadors were, of course, as different from one another as are the countries they represented; one of the fascinations of life in the EEC is the real and continuing diversity of the cultures, attitudes and perspectives of its member states. But within COREPER there was a remarkable sense of shared objectives. Each of my colleagues would argue tenaciously and sometimes tediously for whatever national objective he (sic) was pursuing. But we all knew that if he came to realise either that his approach was flawed in some respect, or that he had no hope of achieving his objective, he would seek instructions to adopt a different line. There was a shared ambition to achieve agreement, if that was possible, in recognition of a shared interest in doing so. There was a remarkable lack of any animosity and indeed a readiness to help or at least not to hassle a colleague who had difficult instructions to carry out. The UK was seen at that early stage in our member-ship as a welcome member and my reception by my colleagues from the other countries was wholly friendly. Meetings could often be long and argumenta-tive; but afterwards there was little, if any, trace of resentment. Even when, with the change of British government in 1974, we started on the irksome (to our partners) task of 'renegotiation', there was a significant degree of under-standing shown to us; and if I sometimes encountered irritation, I never felt hostility.

The atmosphere amongst ministers in the Council was rather different. Disagreement sometimes produced sharper and more aggressive reactions from other ministers. This was partly because they came from different political families, partly because they saw each other less frequently, and partly resulted from their perceived need—all too often for domestic political reasons—to demonstrate publicly how tough they had been. But just as often ministers from different countries became friendly with each other, frequently seeking allies in whatever course they were trying to pursue.

Domestic politics have indeed always been a significant factor shaping British attitudes towards and behaviour within the EC/EU. This is, of course, true of other countries, but in the British case it has been a particularly evident and complicating phenomenon. Membership of the Community, after the successful conclusion of the negotiations in 1972 by the government of Edward Heath, was endorsed by a large parliamentary majority. But it was contested by the opposition Labour party on the grounds that too many concessions had been made in order to reach agreement; and, when Labour returned to power in 1974, it made continuing British membership of the EC dependent on the 'renegotiation' of the terms of entry to which I have already referred. However paradoxical this might seem (given that it was a Labour government under Harold Wilson that had, in 1967, renewed the British application for member-ship, only to be turned down once again by General de Gaulle), it simply reflected the continuing mood of uncertainty about European integration that characterised British public opinion.

The 1975 referendum, with its decisive endorsement of British membership, seemed to have laid that uncertainty to rest. But, over the years since then, there has been a continuing groundswell of opposition to European integration within both of the main political parties and in large sections of the media (much of it owned by foreigners opposed to the EC/EU). This certainly complicated to some extent my own task in Brussels, at least after the 1974 election. But, more importantly, it has made it very difficult for British officials working with Community institutions since then to be as effective and straightforward as they need to be if British interests are to be successfully advanced in EU affairs. It is inevitably damaging to those interests if Britain is continually perceived by our fellow members to be uncertain about its commitment to European integration.

To conclude, I should mention one final issue—almost a detail, yet politically significant nonetheless—which first arose during my time in Brussels. During their talks in Paris, Mr Heath had promised President Pompidou that Britain would not deliberately attempt to undermine the dominance of the French language within the EC—a dominance that had been evident from the outset of the Community, and to which the French attached great importance. When we joined, meetings of the Commission and COREPER were all conducted in French, and the first drafts of all documents were written in French. This was obviously convenient in practical terms, especially for French officials and ministers and French speakers generally. Accordingly, my team and I were under instructions to be able and willing to conduct proceedings and negotiations in French—which I think most of us were able to do. However, when we began to take part in the various meetings, we found that the Irish and the Danes—who had joined at the same time as we—did not intend to speak in French at the meetings, but to conduct their business in English. For a British ambassador, it is hardly possible to decline to speak English at a meeting when a foreign colleague is determined to do so. So we talked English; and I think that was the beginning of the slow process of the erosion of the privileged position of the French language in the conduct of EC business.

1975–1979

DONALD MAITLAND

By way of introduction, and to underline the continuity of personnel that seems to have characterised British EU policy, Michael Palliser refers in the previous section to his presence as an interpreter at the critical meeting between Heath and Pompidou on 21 May 1971. On the same day, as Press Secretary to Prime Minister Edward Heath, I was standing side by side with Denis Baudouin, my French opposite number, in the adjoining room—the Salon des Fêtes in the Elysée Palace in Paris. The Salon was full to capacity with members of the international press. It was in this very Salon ten years earlier that President Charles de Gaulle had pronounced his veto on the admission of the United Kingdom to the then European Economic Community. A hush fell when President Pompidou led the Prime Minister into the Salon. Pompidou stepped forward and pronounced the fateful words:

there are those who take the view that the British are quite unsuited for membership of the European Community. There are also those who believe that France is firmly opposed to British entry. You see in front of you two men who are convinced of the contrary.

The applause was very loud, and the occasion most moving. From where I was standing I could see that there were few dry eyes in the Salon.

In my early years in the Diplomatic Service my responsibilities related for the most part to British interests in the Middle East and relations between the Foreign Office and the media. Subsequently, first as spokesman and then as Principal Private Secretary to two Foreign Secretaries in the 1960s, I attended meetings of the foreign ministers and heads of government of the member states of what was then the European Economic Community. What I learned during those years about Community procedures, and about relations between the member states and between their foreign ministers, provided me with useful background information. However, it was not until later that I was able to appreciate the strength of the fraternal relationship that bound together the Permanent Representatives of the member states, holders of this unique office that required us not only to protect and further the interests of our respective capitals but also—at the same time—to play a full part in the development of European integration.

I took up my post as Sir Michael's successor in Brussels in October 1975. The staff of the United Kingdom Representation to the European Economic Community, as it was called when I arrived there, included representatives from the major Whitehall departments with interests in the future development of Western Europe. The Ministry of Agriculture was well represented, given the special characteristics of the task of creating a Common Agricultural

Policy. The Treasury, Department of Trade and Foreign Office were also strongly represented.

In my first few weeks I thought it would be helpful to all members of the staff of UKRep if we reviewed our objectives, since the United Kingdom was due to assume the Presidency of the Council of Ministers for the first time in January 1977. The six months of the United Kingdom's first Presidency of the Council proved to be an important learning experience not only for the staff of UKRep in Brussels but also for those in Whitehall involved in European Community affairs with whom I discussed events in Brussels every Friday morning at the Cabinet Office in London.

At the end of this intense period of activity in the Community we had made substantial progress in certain fields. We had opened a debate on the next enlargement of the Community. We had secured the Council's endorsement of the accession of Portugal. We had also persuaded the Council to adopt the value added tax directive, and settled a dispute with Iceland over fisheries. Perhaps more importantly, we had shown that the duties of the Presidency could be conducted efficiently and expeditiously. That was certainly the tone of the letters that I received from all my colleagues when our Presidency came to an end. I believe that the fact that the preparations for this, our first presidency, had been in hand for the preceding six months was the main reason for this successful outcome. And it was an outcome that strengthened the already close link between London and UKRep.

During my four years in Brussels I found that the role of Permanent Representative, although onerous, was in many respects unexpectedly rewarding. It was obviously essential to cultivate and maintain good working relations with the representatives of the other member states and key members of the Commission, and especially the President and his senior staff. This occasionally entailed briefing them in strict confidence about the problems London might have with a legislative proposal that came before the Council for consideration. On no occasion during those four years was my confidence breached. On the contrary, I found that certain key Commissioners—notably Ortoli, Haferkamp and Jenkins—invariably expressed appreciation for any confidence shared. These contacts were never mentioned even when the Permanent Representatives met informally, it being understood that confidential consultations of this kind were often instrumental in removing obstacles to progress.

Throughout the years of our membership the role of the press has obviously been of major importance. During my years in Brussels, I had no occasion to complain to any member of the press about any particular report. On the contrary, I found several of the correspondents consistently helpful in providing me with valuable and otherwise inaccessible information.

As for the effect of the trends of public opinion in the United Kingdom on our work, while noting these carefully, we in the UK Representation adopted the policy of speaking openly and frankly and of explaining to all concerned, and especially to the representatives of the press—both British and international—the significance of what we were doing in the national as well as the

© The Political Quarterly Publishing Co. Ltd. 2004

Community interest. Mine were the early days and ministers and the staff of UKRep, with the support of our colleagues in London, sought to convey to the public at home the importance we attached to our belated membership of the Community, despite the opposition of certain sections of the national press. By comparison, political attitudes in today's quite different circumstances are, for the most part, significantly—and understandably—less ambitious.

In October 1979 I was transferred back to London.

1979–1985

MICHAEL BUTLER

By the time I arrived at UKRep as Permanent Representative in 1979, I was already an old European Community hand. I had been taken to Paris by Sir Pierson Dixon (Ambassador in Paris and Deputy to Sir Edward Heath in the first entry negotiations) in 1961 to be his aide in those negotiations. Macmillan, then Prime Minister, had had the mistaken idea that the Ambassador would be able to fix a deal with General de Gaulle or his staff if he was also the head of the official team. The idea was mistaken on two counts. First, the General had no intention of doing a deal with us—though he would have found it harder to veto our entry while he still had no majority in the National Assembly. The second reason, linked to the first, was that the senior official on the delegation ought to have spent half his time or more in London helping Heath to move Whitehall along faster on secondary issues like imports of kangaroo meat. As it was, we applied for membership on 31 July 1961 and had made minimal progress a year later. By the autumn of 1962, when we were ready to get down to business, the General had won elections and a referendum on a new constitution and was in an impregnable position at home. I never forgot the lesson that it was vital to get Whitehall's support for a negotiable position on subjects big and small and to get it in good time from the point of view of the situation in the negotiations in Brussels.

My next direct involvement with what is now the EU was when I returned to London in June 1972 as Head of the European Integration Department dealing with the Community in the Foreign Office when we were preparing to join in January 1973, and when the machinery of the Community for dealing with foreign affairs (political cooperation) was in formation. During the next seven years I was to learn a lot about handling the Whitehall machine. The secret formula was to ensure that the Permanent Representative in Brussels, the senior official in the FCO dealing with the EU and the head of the European coordination staff in the Cabinet Office were in close contact and, if possible, a step ahead of the game, with the London team seeking ministerial instructions in good time.

I was made Under-Secretary at the Foreign Office just in time to be responsible for the so-called renegotiation of the terms of entry at the beginning of 1974. It certainly was a bad moment in our relations with the other member states, but I was dispatched by Jim Callaghan, the Foreign Secretary, on a tour of the member states to stress that we were keen to make the negotiations a success and to stay in the EC. And things improved steadily up to the European Council in Dublin in March 1975.

Thus, when I arrived in Brussels as Permanent Representative I already knew a lot of the players and was familiar with the workings of the system. My first task, in late October 1979, was to give notice to my colleagues in COREPER that, at the forthcoming meeting of European Heads of State and Government in Dublin in November, Mrs Thatcher was going to raise the question of the excessive British net budget contribution. I also faced the problem of convincing them that she meant business. At that stage, the other Permanent Representatives were far from convinced that she did, though their attitudes changed dramatically after her press conference in Dublin, at which she declared that she 'wanted our money back'. Subsequently, they became both more realistic and increasingly annoyed! It was not surprising that her speeches caused upset. They ran contrary to the dogma—so carefully fostered by the French—that 'own resources' were not national contributions and therefore that there was no such thing as a net contribution. Yet, of course, they all knew in their heart of hearts that she had a good case. The trouble was that if the UK was going to pay less, they would all have to either take less or pay more! In retrospect I believe that, had the other member states negotiated in a more friendly and positive spirit at the beginning of 1980, they could have achieved what they did in 1984 without the need for the constant arguments that were a feature of the four years during which we were negotiating.

One characteristic of COREPER is that its members know each other very well. Thus, although what they say officially has to be in accordance with their instructions, they can—unofficially—be more inventive in trying to ease their way towards solutions. Even at the worst moments of the British budget campaign, most of the other members of COREPER were perfectly friendly to me, and our professional and personal relations did not suffer. It is significant, for example, that when the Falklands War broke out in 1982 (at a very difficult stage in the budget negotiations), COREPER was able to agree in only two meetings that there should be a complete boycott of Argentine goods.

COREPER lunches were an important part of life. They took place every Thursday and Roy Jenkins, then the President of the European Commission, attended once a month. During the early stage of the budget negotiations Roy felt it was his duty to give me a hard time. The others must have thought me pretty tiresome, as I stuck politely by my line and my instructions—partly because I believed in them, partly too because I would have been sacked very quickly had I not done so! That earned me a description I have always treasured—from the *Financial Times*, no less. The *FT* ran a profile of me in which they described me as 'persistent to the point of tiresomeness'. When his country needs to get its way, that is what a Permanent Representative has to be!

In the final stages of the budgetary negotiations, before Fontainebleau in 1984, I was able to use a COREPER lunch to clear away the vital technical obstacle of how our excessive contribution should be measured. The words 'net contribution' remained anathema to the other member states, but the formula of 'the gap between our VAT share and our expenditure share' was finally accepted after I had privately persuaded the Germans to put it forward. It was a difference more of words than of substance. That is the sort of sort of initiative that a Permanent Representative has to take from time to time.

In those days the European Parliament (EP) had much less power than it does now. But I used to go down to Strasbourg every month and brief the Conservative and Labour members of the European Parliament (MEPs) until, one day, Barbara Castle—at the time the leader of the Labour Group in the EP—informed me that the Labour MEPs were so hostile to both the European Community and Margaret Thatcher that they no longer wished to talk to me.

On the subject of the Prime Minister, my previous experience had certainly helped prepare me for the arduous routine of Councils and COREPER meetings, and for working with the Cabinet Office and the other departments on Fridays to prepare my instructions for the following weeks. It had not, however, prepared me for Mrs Thatcher, and particularly for the late night discussions with her at European Council meetings. In Stuttgart in 1983, for example, she summoned me in the early hours and, having consumed several whiskies and sounded off about the iniquities of both her colleagues and the European Community in general, turned to me at 3 am and said: 'All right, Michael, draft something for me to say tomorrow and we'll look at it at breakfast. Breakfast at 7.' Of course, I did as she asked—and a very good discussion we had at breakfast. She then went off—apparently impervious to the effects of either the alcohol or the sleeplessness—and negotiated a crucial and constructive declaration that eased our way to success in the budget negotiations over the course of the next year.

The press have always represented us as having worse relations with our colleagues in the European Community than has actually been the case. Handling the journalists was never easy and Bernard Ingham, Margaret Thatcher's spokesman, always wanted to make the European Council sound like a battlefield on which her colleagues were routed. The press tended to ignore all the constructive work done in COREPER and its numerous working groups, without which there would have been no agreement on legislation. My world class team of officials, one-third from the FCO and two-thirds from other Whitehall departments, worked very closely with me. But the press, with honourable exceptions, did not really want to know that hours of patient work in the groups had produced solutions with which everyone was fairly happy. Normally, EU negotiations are not a zero-sum game in which there are absolute winners and losers. The skill of the officials is to use their inventive and persuasive powers to craft a solution that suits everyone. That doesn't make a good headline.

I believe the norm in terms of Britain's relations with the EC/EU has been constructive engagement. The single market was very largely a British creation. We launched the movement to complete the single market at the European Council in 1983 and were able to convert the first Intergovernmental Conference (IGC) in 1984/85 into a preparation for the 1985 Single European Act. During my six years we had one or two real rows about the budget in 1979/80 but during my last three years things went fairly smoothly—with one or two minor hiccups, such as when Andreotti, then Italian Prime Minister, ambushed Margaret to set up the first IGC at the European Council in Milan in July 1984. However when we got back to Brussels and I requested, during a

COREPER meeting, that all delegations table a paper setting out what it was they wanted to come out of the conference, the fact that no one produced anything significant left us with the opportunity to give the single market a free run.

I have said very little about relations with the Commission, which form an important part of the job. They have to be managed at every level. Often on some quite important subject it is a rather junior official in the Commission who really counts. My staff and I had to judge at what level any approach would be most likely to produce results. Normally, I would not have gone myself to see officials below the rank of Director-General, except perhaps in the 'private offices' or *cabinets* of the Commissioners themselves. But I would certainly have wanted to be consulted about how the Commission should be handled on any important subject. As for the Commissioners themselves, they varied widely in their capacity to get things done. In my time Stevie Davignon of Belgium was by far the most effective member of the Commission and I often went to discuss important current issues with him rather than with one of the two British Commissioners.

Being a Permanent Representative is not always conducive to a civilised life. Meetings, especially of the Council, where the ministers all feel the need to make speeches that will be reported positively in their national media, tend to be boring and to go on for far too long. How many times would I say to my wife in the morning that I expected that the Foreign Secretary and his small team, or another minister, would want to come home to dinner, but that she had better have the cook prepare something cold because it was impossible to predict when the meeting would end. Then at about 7 pm I would send her a message from the Council that we wouldn't be back till nine, but still hoped to dine at home. Then, when the Council Secretariat—an admirable and underrated body—started bringing round the whisky at about 8.30 and there were still tricky points to be settled, I knew that we would get nothing but the dreaded sandwiches at the Council table that night and I would creep out to tell my wife that the dinner could be put away.

So perhaps it was no wonder that after six years I thought I had done my duty by the nation and sought permission to retire early. I had done the things in the EC that I needed to do and wanted to earn some money to supplement my pension. Geoffrey Howe—then Foreign Secretary, and someone I had known since school—was sympathetic, but said I would have to go and talk to the Prime Minister. So I did and in the end she graciously agreed. But she made it clear that she simply could not understand how I could choose not to be at the centre of things by her side. It seemed to me that she was thinking more of her own future than of mine!

⏴ The Political Quarterly Publishing Co. Ltd. 2004

1985–1990

DAVID HANNAY

Like those who preceded me, and to a growing degree, British ambassadors arrive in Brussels with significant experience of European integration. I am the only Permanent Representative to date, however, who served for four years in the European Commission prior to joining UKRep. I joined the Commission in 1973 with Christopher Soames, as his *chef de cabinet*. The experience was invaluable in preparing me to deal not only with my Permanent Representative colleagues, but also with Commissioners and their officials who are, all too often, neither particularly well treated nor particularly well understood by the Permanent Representatives. Before joining the Commission, I had already spent eight years in Brussels in the UK delegation, the last two of these as part of the negotiating team working on the terms of the UK's accession.

When I took up my post as Permanent Representative in October 1985, the agenda of the European Community had effectively been set by three events: the settlement at Fontainebleau in 1984, which had produced a self-executing abatement mechanism for dealing with the British budget contribution; the decision to admit Spain and Portugal, due to be implemented on 1 January 1986; and, by far the most operationally important, the decision taken at Milan in June 1985 to set up an Intergovernmental Conference to undertake the first ever major revision of the Rome Treaties. The Conference, which was in full swing by the time I arrived, was focused principally on two issues: first, the White Paper on the Single Market that Jacques Delors and Arthur Cockfield had tabled shortly beforehand; second, on giving a Treaty base to foreign policy cooperation for the first time.

For all the sound and fury amidst which I arrived, due to Mrs Thatcher having been voted down in Milan on the original decision to call an Intergovernmental Conference, the European Community was, in fact, taking two substantial steps towards what could reasonably be called a British agenda. The two main items being negotiated—the single market and foreign policy cooperation—were both at the heart of successive British governments' aspirations for the European Community. Other issues, such as Economic and Monetary Union, were left to one side for the time being.

Things continued to go well for the two years after the successful completion of the IGC. The Single Market legislative programme began to roll through the Council. The provision for qualified majority voting proved to be the key to the creation of a single market on the liberal, deregulatory terms that Britain wanted. One only has to look at the banking directive, where the Germans were voted down, to see how that worked out in practice. The benefits from the Single Market programme began to boost the economies of all the member states.

Then in 1987/8 the Single European Act was followed by the successful conclusion of a marathon set of budgetary negotiations, known as the Delors Package. This introduced, for the first time, measures to reform the CAP, and to control spending on it, and also maintained the British abatement. It also included a massive increase in structural fund spending. And, for the first time, it set out a clear medium-term framework and figures for all European spending. The upper revenue limit of 1.27% of GNP was established, and remains to this day.

I am afraid to say that, from then on, it was downhill all the way for the rest of my tenure in Brussels as far as Britain was concerned. The Bruges speech of September 1988 was a sad story for which I have to accept some responsibility. I thought at the time that it was important that, after all those years of battling on budgetary and other matters, the British government should set out its views on the future of European integration in positive terms. I persuaded the Prime Minister that it would be a good idea to come to Bruges to do just that. It was at that point that I lost control over what went into the speech, as did John Kerr (my eventual successor in Brussels), who was then the Under-Secretary at the Foreign Office dealing with the EC. The speech certainly caused uproar with its forthright criticism of the EC institutions. It is, however, worth remembering that half of it was taken up by a magnificent cry for an enlarged Europe to include central and eastern Europe. Mrs Thatcher was almost the only person at that stage actually looking towards that enlarged European Union, which finally came into being this year. She was at the time the only national leader who said (and I paraphrase) 'Don't forget that Warsaw, Prague and Budapest are European cities just as much as are London and Paris and Rome.' That was an act of vision for which she is given little credit.

All that, alas, was lost amidst the furore caused by the Prime Minister's onslaught in the rest of the speech on the Commission and the other European institutions and her negative attitude towards any further integration. From then onwards, the gathering pace in Brussels towards Economic and Monetary Union caused a lot of trouble for the UK because we adopted a policy of denial rather than one of discussion and negotiation. The decision at Hanover in 1988 to set up the Delors Committee of central bankers turned out to be, not as Mrs Thatcher unwisely hoped, a touchstone for EMU, but rather its launching pad. As I left UKRep, the Maastricht intergovernmental conferences were getting under way and, three months later, Mrs Thatcher resigned. We were already moving steadily towards the opt-out on EMU, which was the eventual outcome.

This bleak period in Britain's relationship with Europe was compounded by Mrs Thatcher's aberrant attitude towards German unification. She wanted to use the European Community to place obstacles in the path of unification. Eventually, however, this tactic had the undesirable effect of driving the French and Germans even closer together, following Mitterrand's initial flirtation with her opposition to unification.

Public and political opinion in Britain during this period were less problematic than one might have expected, and for three reasons. First, the Labour

© The Political Quarterly Publishing Co. Ltd. 2004

party was even more negative about European integration than the Conservative party is now, though it did begin, particularly with Jacques Delors's appearance at the TUC conference in 1988, to climb out of the hole that it had got into when it committed itself in its 1983 election manifesto to withdrawal. So, while our partners might not have liked Mrs Thatcher much, they wanted a Labour government even less. Secondly, the Tory eurosceptics were somewhat cowed by the fact that Mrs Thatcher was in charge. It was not terribly easy to accuse Mrs Thatcher of being soft on Europe, whatever they may have thought. And thirdly the press was more positive than negative. We did not then have that solid block of the Black, Murdoch and Rothermere presses going full steam all the time, with which my successors now have to contend.

Commission President Jacques Delors was perplexed by the difficulties he had in dealing with Mrs Thatcher, and saddened by the aggressive tone of the British press. He never believed you could build Europe without Britain. Increasingly, however, he saw us as an obstacle around which he would have to navigate, rather than as an active partner in the European project.

The attitudes of our European partners towards us were a combination of irritation, of respect and, when Mrs Thatcher herself was on the scene, of a certain amount of fear. She was after all a big beast in the European jungle and her presence at the European Council was a formidable one. It was recognised that our interdepartmental coordination was second to none. And, for a few years, there was real convergence between Britain's European agenda and that of the other member states, although many problems and divergences were stored up for the future. As for COREPER, I agree with those of my colleagues who have said it is a club of professionals who did not let their emotions take over their job, of people who are there to negotiate effectively but dispassionately in the national interest. They managed to do so, in my experience, without calling each other names or falling out with each other. Its working was never adversely affected by the spats that were going on between our political leaders.

1990–1995

JOHN KERR

I replaced David Hannay in the summer of 1990. Sending me to Brussels was therefore one of Mrs Thatcher's last European decisions, and John Major was Prime Minister for most of my five years in post there.

It was Michael Palliser, whose Private Secretary I was during his time as Permanent Under-Secretary at the Foreign Office, who first aroused my interest in EC affairs. My direct involvement began when I was in the Treasury, and, as the Chancellor's Private Secretary, attended both ECOFIN Councils and ERM realignment meetings (of which there were many) between 1981 and 1984. I had also been EC Under-Secretary in the FCO from 1987 to 1990, attending all European Council and General Affairs Council meetings, and learning from watching David Hannay in action. Theoretically he got his instructions from me: debating them with him was almost as demanding as with Mrs Thatcher, though the 'friendly fire' tended to come from the opposite direction. Stephen Wall and Nigel Sheinwald were in my FCO team: the latter, along with John Grant, completed my education when we worked together in UKRep.

I enjoyed my time as Permanent Representative. It was probably the most intellectually demanding job I ever did.[18] But much of it was negotiating—and negotiating is my addiction. It becomes obsessive. You are Whitehall's barrister, making Whitehall's case in Brussels, and the *sine qua non* is to know, really know, Whitehall's brief. Not just what they want, but why they want it. No matter how technical the subject, no matter how brilliant your backroom team, you need to know the files yourself if you are to have the confidence to make the case in your own words, as for effectiveness you must. So you burn the midnight oil. And you badger Whitehall, where your credibility depends not just on delivering the goods, by hook, crook or fluke, but on demonstrably knowing their stuff. So you are in London for a full day every week, using the time difference to be in their offices before they are, falling asleep by Harrods on the evening drive back out to Heathrow.

UKRep has to be embedded in Whitehall, and seen by Whitehall as their outpost in Brussels: it must not be, and never has been, seen as an outpost of Brussels in London. The negotiator needs to have the authority back home to enable him to seize the midnight negotiating opportunity, when an opponent blinks or the story takes an unexpected twist. And the visiting minister is more likely to accept tactical advice if he knows that his strategic aim is understood.

Longevity also helps. I think we are right to send our negotiators for long spells. I had three French and five Greek counterparts. By the time I left, only the Belgian had been there longer. Longevity confers a spurious but useful authority. My Belgian colleague and I became adept at debating precedent across the COREPER table. On the (rare) occasions when our policy aims coincided, we could be incontrovertibly, and sometimes imaginatively, precise and pertinent in our recollections. Analysing other countries' policies— essential when one has the Presidency, as we did in 1992—is important at all times. So is getting to know their negotiators, their virtues, vanities and vulnerabilities. Alliance-building, and a bit of timely help to a new colleague, pays off, for multilateral diplomacy is rarely a zero-sum game, and a favour done, at no cost to the UK, can provide future benefits for the country.

In those days there was a real camaraderie in COREPER, perhaps more so than today. Yet one must not exaggerate, as UK eurosceptics then often did, and imagine a sinister cabal is building a common European structure behind governments' backs. I remember how even certain senior cabinet ministers flirted with this theory, and how irritating I found it, after days of COREPER combat, to defend their policies. An anecdote captures their suspicion and my irritation. One of my colleagues, a man of great talent and charm but concerned for his health had, on a previous posting in Peru, acquired an elegant full-length black alpaca cloak that he would from time to time wear in COREPER or the Council, to ward off dangerous draughts. Spotting the cloak, and feeling tetchy, the senior minister alongside me asked what on earth it was. Also tetchy, and cross about the COREPER cabal theory, I replied that it was standard COREPER uniform. The joke fell flat. Within a week a grave and senior official of the same department came to ask, on instructions, how much my COREPER uniform had cost the taxpayer.

COREPER's workload was rather different then. Compared to today, there was proportionately much less foreign policy on the agenda. Conversely, there was much more coordination, for the General Affairs Council then lived up to its name, not limiting itself to Foreign Affairs, and COREPER, as its official-level counterpart, negotiated on issues ranging from institutional affairs (particularly in the year of Maastricht), to EU finances (particularly in the run up to John Major's Edinburgh tour-de-force), to structural fund allocations, to Coal and Steel Treaty measures, to enlargement terms—and, of course, fish, forever fish. Whether in a Common Fisheries Policy or Norwegian or Canadian context, the last crisis of every term seemed always to be about fish. The only time I had to spend Easter Sunday in COREPER, we were talking Grand Banks cod.

We also, moreover, did much more internal EC legislation than COREPER does today. I was in Brussels in the period described by David Hannay, in which a mass of Single Market law was passing through the Council. Much of it came via COREPER I, where my colleagues and deputies, the three brilliant Davids—Elliott, Durie and Bostock—almost certainly worked harder than I did, but the Permanent Representative then handled the ECOFIN, Energy and Industry Councils, more than half of whose agenda was legislation, as well as the General Affairs and Development Councils and the European Council.

This, of course, has changed, as John Grant points out in his contribution to this collection. Legislation is no longer the negotiator's core function. When back in Brussels as the Convention Secretary-General in 2002–3, I was struck by the retreat from the concept that European integration is best built on ever wider EU powers and an ever bigger EU statute book. That tide has turned: Maastricht was probably its high water mark. Those in the Convention arguing the old Commission case on both points were a small minority, whereas they had been in the majority at Maastricht, and stopping them was a Major priority.

By 2002, mindsets in the institutions had also changed in other ways. Economic 'liberalism' is now a dirty word in only one European language. *Dirigisme* is out of fashion; and the virtues of centralised economic planning have even less resonance among the states from Eastern Europe that have now recently joined the Union. There is something real behind the rhetoric of the Lisbon Agenda, and about trying to become more competitive without adopting a standardised single blueprint. Competition between systems is no longer seen as morally disreputable. All this has served to make the EU more UK-friendly.

So, too, does language. I joined a COREPER in which the majority language—indeed the exclusive language when working without inter-preters—was French. When I left, it was English. I remember French consternation when, at the first meeting with the ten countries of Eastern Europe plus Cyprus and Malta, eleven spoke in English, and only one (the Romanian) in French. The big change had occurred with the EFTAn enlargement: when the Swedes and Finns elected to use English in COREPER and the Council, the balance tilted decisively. The Austrian might have tried to use German, as German Permanent Representatives, on orders from home, did from time to time, but the attempt failed when my French colleague (who naturally spoke perfect German), leapt to his feet complaining that he couldn't understand a word that was being said. Spanish insistence on parity with any concession to German didn't help Bonn either. But the French defence of their language against all-comers has failed. Even the Commission now works in English.

While Brussels has become more UK-friendly, the reverse is not universally the case. Certainly, Whitehall's EU expertise has grown immensely. Take the Home Office. Before Maastricht that great Department of State barely knew that the EC existed; but when the UK government drew up its Convention negotiating aims, who came forward with the most imaginative proposals? A Home Office fed up with the inefficiency of the Third Pillar, and wanting more decisive action, with qualified majority voting on issues such as asylum and immigration. Only Treasury mindsets are slow to change: most of Whitehall now willingly boards the Brussels Eurostar, seeing more opportunities than threats over there.

The same, however, cannot be said of Westminster. Attempts to scrutinise draft EU legislation, and cross-examine Whitehall or the Commission, still do not engage the full attention of the House of Commons, though the House of Lords tries harder. New opportunities for closer involvement are on offer in the Draft Constitutional Treaty: whether Westminster will seize them is unclear. Carping from the sidelines, or after the event, is easier. Moreover, even the serious UK newspapers, while happy to complain that much UK legislation derives from EU law, ignore the European Parliament's prior legislative process. The powers of the EP relative to the other EU institutions have grown greatly since my day (and today's Permanent Representatives rightly spend much more time in the European Parliament than did I); but the UK press hasn't noticed.

Much of our press still prefers EU fiction to EU fact. The needle is still stuck in the old groove. It fell to me to explain to Jacques Delors the *Sun's* treatment of him: not easy. Mind you, one could occasionally turn nonsense to advantage. When I had to persuade Vice-President Bangemann, a man of great weight in the Delors Commission, that he should drop a proposal to outlaw an additive apparently essential to the UK sausage, I found that the diplomatic technique that worked best was to present him with a nice volume of his UK press cuttings, giving pride of place to the front-page picture headlined 'Big Bangers Is After Ours'. Perhaps former public servants should do more to counter the damaging press euroscepticism. But would we carry much weight? I doubt it, because the public service tradition in this country has kept us out of the public gaze. Certainly, the EU deserves to be criticised, and often, but not always; and it would really need government spokesmen to lead on setting the record straight if the criticism isn't always to be believed.

Since I went to COREPER, the UK government's tone towards the European Union has changed twice, in 1990 and in 1997. The first change, though not long-lasting, was productive. Mrs Thatcher's approach to Monetary Union had been to preach against it, because she deeply believed that it would not work. Mr Major spotted that it would go ahead, and that if we blocked its introduction on an EU-wide basis it would still go ahead, in a smaller group in which we would have no seat and no say. Messina all over again, in other words. So our Maastricht aim was to ensure that we did have a say, could ensure that monetary union took a UK-friendly form, and would have a ticket of entry should we ever decide to join. That aim was seen as constructive; and it was achieved. But as the Conservative party's split on Europe deepened in the mid-1990s and the tone of the government's contribution to domestic debate on Europe soured, it became harder to seem constructive, and less was achieved. Then came 1997, and a Blair government which engaged actively, with enthusiasm, and refreshingly constructively in EU debate, taking the time to make contacts, build partnerships and propose initiatives. It seems to me that this has brought real dividends, but now needs to be taken further. But that may entail the government being as positive and engaged in the domestic exposition of its EU policies as it is in their pursuit, so far rather successful, in Brussels.

1995–2000

STEPHEN WALL

When I went to Brussels in 1995 it was the first time I had worked directly with the EU institutions. I had, however, spent five years in the mid-1980s as head of one of the Foreign Office's two European departments, handling the British rebate and the Single European Act. As Private Secretary to Geoffrey Howe, Douglas Hurd and John Major, I had 'lived' most of the subsequent big EU negotiations, including Maastricht. As Ambassador in Lisbon I had learned to see the EU through the eyes of a smaller member state benefiting hugely from the Union's cohesion policies.

The UK Representation in Brussels that I joined in 1995 was a hundred-strong negotiating machine made up of the brightest, mostly young, people from across Whitehall. It was very unhierarchical. I worked directly with the expert on each subject. The lines of command were short but heavily loaded. I was required to get my head round a huge number of technical issues, many of which were also political timebombs domestically. In the election year of 1997, when I was the negotiator on the Amsterdam Treaty, my instructions changed from 'Just say no' to 'Start saying yes' between 30 April and a week later. The emphasis of the job became one of projecting, as well as protecting, British interests.

The bulk of my work was in the negotiations on individual bits of EU legislation in COREPER. It was important to have a clear remit from London on the policy objective, combined with maximum freedom of manoeuvre on the tactics of getting there. COREPER is something of a club: all its members have more or less difficult instructions to fulfil. They want both to win their own points and to help others. Managing the balance between the two is one of the tricks of the trade. But the UK Permanent Representation has many other ports of call than COREPER. The first is the Commission—seeking to influence proposals before they see the light of day as well as at every subsequent stage. The second is the European Parliament.

One of the big changes that occurred during my time was the enormous growth of the co-decision procedure, a new decision making process introduced by the Maastricht treaty and expanded to cover more policy areas at subsequent IGCs. Without going into the horrendously technical details of the procedure, suffice to say that it entailed a significant increase in the power of the European Parliament over decision making. COREPER is an important institution but not, in my view, a powerful one. The powerful institutions remain the Council (for which COREPER carries out the preparatory work), the Commission and the European Parliament. The European Parliament's power has grown enormously, partly because of co-decision and partly as a consequence of the demise of the Commission over the course of the last decade or so.

Turning to more political issues, I attended a debate between Hugo Young and Michael Portillo shortly after Hugo had published his great book about Britain and European integration.[19] When Michael Portillo came to reply to Hugo's argument—that Britain should have been more positively engaged than it had been—he argued that Hugo had not taken sufficiently into account the constraints of public opinion and parliamentary majorities on successive British governments. These constraints are certainly one of the enduring features of recent relations between the UK and EU, and they were prevalent during my time in Brussels.

However, I would argue that there have never been anti-European British governments. We have had anti-European oppositions; and we have had governments that have been very much constrained by public opinion and by their own domestic situation. Yet the examples mentioned by my predecessors are revelatory. Harold Wilson and Jim Callaghan undertook the renegotiation of Britain's terms of entry referred to by Donald Maitland and Michael Butler in this collection in order to keep us in the European Community. Margaret Thatcher's stance during the negotiations over the Single European Act was certainly designed to produce an outcome that suited British interests, but it also involved a significant concession over something she regarded as a pretty firm principle via the introduction of qualified majority voting.

John Major, meanwhile, has been much criticised for claiming game, set and match after Maastricht. Yet he was actually acting against his better judgement. He did not believe that economic union was the right prescription for the European Union, yet he was allowing the rest of our partners to go ahead while Britain stayed out and in so doing, as John Kerr points out, maximised British influence over, and minimised Britain's marginalisation from, the process. So, far from this being a 'blocking' agenda by the United Kingdom, it was one where Britain accommodated what the government saw as the national interest to the wider European interest.

I experienced, from Brussels, a period when the constraints on a British government were extremely tight, namely the period of non-cooperation over BSE. It has been said by some (including by at least one of my predecessors at UKRep) that the policy infuriated our partners. I saw it slightly differently. First of all, we had a British government with no majority in the House of Commons and enough backbenchers prepared to vote it down, to the extent that it did not know at any moment whether it could carry its own policies or not. Second, we were faced with a crisis in the agricultural sector of proportions that no previous British government had ever had to contend with. The then agricultural minister was talking to his colleagues in terms of the possibility that the whole of the British herd might have to be destroyed. Finally, we confronted the closure of our European market.

Given all this, how was the government to demonstrate to its partners that this was an issue of the most fundamental political importance? Faced with these numerous problems, it took a decision whose ramifications it probably had not thought through—namely the policy of non-cooperation—and rapidly thereafter came to the conclusion that this was not a viable policy to pursue.

28

Hence noncooperation was abandoned within a relatively short period. The other side of the coin, however, was that our partners also realised that it was necessary to construct a framework that would enable us both to end non-cooperation and, more importantly, to do what we had failed to do, which was to construct a serious scientific framework within which we as a country and the European Union as a whole could tackle the BSE crisis. The fact that this happened is actually an enormous tribute to Jacques Santer, much maligned though he is, and, if I may say so, to Neil Kinnock and Leon Brittan, the two British Commissioners at the time who helped steer the framework through.

That was for me the most vivid example of a government struggling with the constraints of domestic pressures on the one hand while nonetheless trying, according to its lights, to make a success of our membership. By the time Labour won the 1997 election, we had reached a point—and this is where the Major government differed from its predecessors—where our partners had begun to ask themselves whether it was possible for the British government to sustain its commitment to the basic precepts of membership. Obviously, they saw a completely different approach when Labour came in. They also saw, however—and it is a point which is less obvious to us as we see things through the prism of the platforms of the various parties—a fundamental continuity of British policy on issues such as external trade, CAP reform, the single market and economic reform. Indeed, on the last issue John Major came to Brussels shortly before the election and made a speech about the economic reform agenda in terms quite similar to those that Tony Blair has subsequently used. However, because of the political situation the speech achieved no broader resonance. By trying to be proactive in building alliances, we have subsequently been able to get some resonance behind a programme of economic reform which otherwise would not have been possible.

If I have learned one lesson from my involvement in European Union business, it is the enormous advantage to be gained from making a real effort to have constructive relationships with our partners. This is something that Whitehall is much better at than it was twenty years ago. It enables us to build alliances and hence to reinforce our chances of promoting our positive agenda. It also provides us with friends when we need them, particularly on those occasions when we are confronted with something that we find genuinely unacceptable.

2000–2003

NIGEL SHEINWALD

I took up the post of Permanent Representative in the summer of 2000, by which time I had had about a dozen years' continuous experience of EU affairs. I had been involved in the Maastricht IGC and the UK's 1992 Presidency from the London end. I then had two years as UKRep Head of Political and Institutional Affairs (the old 'Head of Chancery' job) in 1993–5. A good deal of my work as Foreign Office Press Secretary in 1995–8 was on European matters. For the two years before going to Brussels as Permanent Representative, I had been Europe Director in the FCO, responsible for all EU issues and the UK's bilateral relations with our EU partners. In that role I had led for the FCO on the Berlin future financing negotiation, enlargement, economic reform and the IGC which concluded in Nice, which was half way through when I started as Permanent Representative. So I felt I was reasonably familiar with current issues when I arrived.

By the summer of 2000, the present government had been in office for three years. Thus the honeymoon period enjoyed by the Blair administration in its relationship with its EU partners was coming to an end. Yet the vast majority of policy people in Brussels recognised that there had been a distinct shift in policy, although some, of course, had hoped that the UK would move further and faster than it did, particularly over the euro. The early part of my posting was characterised by a generally weak Franco-German relationship. Partly as a consequence, London was able to make good use of the kinds of tactical, policy based alliances that Stephen Wall has referred to. I arrived just after the successful Lisbon summit in 2000, in the run up to which we had certainly made use of that technique. This approach had significantly pushed economic reform up the agenda.

At that stage, the UK was comfortably placed in most of the major negotiations under way in Brussels. This was exemplified by European Council meetings. On the final morning of a European Council, the Conclusions text plops onto the mat very early in the morning. Ten years ago there would have been a dozen really horrendous points that would have had to be taken to the Prime Minister (though thankfully not immediately after the kinds of whisky fuelled 3 am meetings to which Michael Butler was subjected). In the recent past, this has not been the case. The set of negotiations that ran through my time in Brussels were those on enlargement, where the UK was able to be the friend of the Commission, of successive Presidencies and of the enlargement countries. On economic reform, the single market, the environment and foreign policy, we managed, for the most part, to lead or at least to be part of the majority. Of course it wasn't always like that. The negotiations over the tax package which dragged on throughout most of Stephen Wall's time and were only concluded in the summer of 2003, proved fraught, particularly in their early stages. Even once there existed a sizeable majority in favour of the British vision of tax transparency, the going remained difficult, not least over the negotiations with Switzerland. In general, however, representing the UK in Brussels was not the permanent war of attrition that some like to suggest.

Much of the British media in particular found this state of affairs both disappointing and unsettling. 'Fourteen versus one' or 'UK isolated' were easy headlines to write, though totally at odds with the reality on the ground. It was consistently difficult to entice the media to pay attention to the longer-term issues such as enlargement and economic competitiveness that were developing steadily according to a largely British agenda.

During my time in Brussels the big issue was of course the relationship between the Europeans and the United States following 11 September 2001 and leading up to the conflict in Iraq. Yet even here my impression is that the British public were given a misleading impression of what was going on in the Union. The UK was not isolated in Brussels over Iraq. There were about six countries of the present 15 in our camp; there were one or two who were with the French and Germans; and the others were in the middle. If you include the Accession 10, it felt very different from the picture portrayed in the UK. Nevertheless, it certainly was a difficult and tense period. The most brittle atmosphere at a European Council that I have ever experienced was that at the meeting held in the run up to the conflict in Iraq in February 2003.

Yet, as others have pointed out, however difficult the atmosphere was at the stratospheric level, professional relationships within COREPER remained pretty normal and were not weakened by these political spats. What did affect COREPER, however, was enlargement. The new members joined us after the signature of the Accession Treaty in April 2003. The increase from 15 to 25 was instantly obvious—microphones at the lunch table; fewer seats per delegation at the negotiating table for Council meetings; a new Code of Conduct, imperfectly applied, to assist business management. It was still early days by the time I left, but some of the intimacy and focus which had previously characterised the workings of COREPER had inevitably already dissipated.

One further obvious change occurred in the nature of the post during my tenure. Previously, COREPER had been the all-consuming centre of a Permanent Representative's life. It was still very important in my time—this was one of the core functions in that only the Permanent Representative could carry it out. But there were differences. First, COREPER's ambit had changed: it had little involvement in the big economic and monetary issues, which were dealt with by the Economic and Financial Committee—although it remained in charge of the budget and financial services. In the external area, it was supported by the Political and Security Committee on pure foreign and defence policy. It acquired, however, a massive new portfolio in Justice and Home Affairs. But the decision to move preparations for the current IGC to the Convention on the Future of Europe deprived COREPER of one of its traditional roles. COREPER remained the most effective negotiating tool in the EU, but its role was less dominant than in the past.

At the same time, the job had also become broader, and came to involve representing the UK to a wider set of constituencies. UKRep is now a more public institution and its outreach is much greater—to stakeholders in the UK, and to the large pool of people in Brussels with an interest in the EU. These include business, NGOs, lawyers, lobbyists, the media and academic organisations. There is a very big British presence in Brussels which, in and of itself, reflects the greater sense of comfort that the British—if not their government or media—feel in their dealings with the European Union.

There are two other developments I should mention. First, devolution. This started in my predecessor's time, and developed in mine. The Brussels experience continues to be a happy one. The heads of the Scottish, Welsh and Northern Ireland Executive Offices and their top staff are part of UKRep, and I brought them regularly into our discussions on the basis of remarkable two-way transparency. At the same time, they had their day-to-day autonomy and links back to their capitals. Of course all this added complexity to our overall British effort in Brussels; but it actually strengthened it, not only by maintaining our single UK negotiating position but also by giving better expression to the specific interests of each part of the UK. Occasionally there were strains, but we managed them.

Second, as my predecessors have mentioned, there was the growing role of the European Parliament. By the time of my arrival, this was just a fact of life. Regular contacts with the British party leaders and leading MEPs, regular grillings by the three main British delegations in Brussels and Strasbourg, and contacts with the President and other senior officers of the Parliament were standard fare for the UK Permanent Representative. The UKRep team became increasingly skilled as negotiators and lobbyists in the Parliament, and promoters in Whitehall of the need to take the EP seriously. I also tried to maintain a good dialogue with our delegations to the Committee of the Regions and the Economic and Social Committee. All this added up to a different, wider role from the negotiation- and COREPER-focused lives of earlier Permanent Representatives.

The only record I set in my three years in Brussels was that I worked directly (and harmoniously and productively) with all three of my immediate predecessors. Stephen Wall—then Head of the European Secretariat in the Cabinet Office—was the person who interrogated me every Friday across the Cabinet Office table. John Kerr, as Permanent Under-Secretary in the Foreign Office, used to come to the big European Council meetings and then returned to Brussels as Secretary General of the Convention on the Future of Europe. David Hannay was a regular visitor as the UK Special Representative on Cyprus. One of the favourite albums of my youth was a live one by Crosby, Stills, Nash and Young. As Stephen Stills said of Neil Young, before one of the tracks, 'we've had our ups and downs, but we're still playing together'.

2003–

JOHN GRANT

When I arrived in Brussels for the first time—in 1989, as Press Spokesman in UKRep—the EU still had 12 member states and frankly it was inconceivable, at the beginning of September of that year, that we would soon be talking about an EFTAn enlargement or Association Agreements with the four Warsaw Pact countries. Three years later I was involved (as a Desk Officer in UKRep's External Relations Section) in the opening of accession negotiations with Sweden, Austria, Finland and Norway; meanwhile, my colleagues were negotiating the arrangements that would pave the way for the entry of the states of Central and Eastern Europe. When I left Brussels in July 1997, to work as Robin Cook's Private Secretary six months ahead of the 1998 UK Presidency (and after three years as Head of UKRep's External Relations Section, preceded by six months at the Cabinet Office's European Secretariat), the EU was on the point of taking the decision to open enlargement negotiations with Poland, the Czech Republic and others.

In terms of process, the move from 12 to 15 was crucial in the way it affected the dynamics of the Council bodies. This has nothing to do either with the identity of the new member states or with any shortcomings anywhere in the system. Rather, and curiously enough, it is simply that the way business is transacted at 12 is very different to the way in which it is done at 15. It follows that we will do business in a different way at 25. Getting business done, as we are already discovering in the Council, in COREPER and in the working groups, will mean a mixture of three things. It will mean some treaty change: the Constitutional Treaty will be relevant to that, but is not the decisive element. It will need a change in working methods—though the extent to which different working methods solve these kinds of problems tends to be overstated by serving bureaucrats.

Most fundamentally, managing to get things done effectively at 25 requires from all involved a different way of thinking about the way we do business. We need to think outside the context of the formal day-to-day negotiations in COREPER if we are to make a success of enlargement. That process is already underway but it will be an increasingly important facet of COREPER's life over the next few years. I am sure COREPER lunches at 9 were an extremely effective forum for doing business. However a COREPER lunch at 25 is not, I imagine, nearly as effective (Nigel Sheinwald has mentioned the fact that there are now microphones on the lunch table). An EU of 25 representatives is a fundamentally different environment in which to operate and I am very struck by that, coming back to Brussels after a gap of 6 years.

Nearly all my predecessors have discussed great projects in their contributions to this volume: the Single European Act was a great project, and a great

British success to boot. Enlargement is a great project, now coming to final fruition and also a great British success. I also think that the incorporation of justice and home affairs represents a great project. The next great project, however, is—and will be—very different. It is neither a legislative nor a treaty based project; it is not about a very complex set of negotiations—as enlargement has been. It is about economic reform and the global competitiveness of the European Union. Previous projects had something in common. John Kerr talks of the Single Market legislation requiring a certain kind of dynamic in the Council and between the various EC institutions, and of the sheer weight of legislation passing through the Council during his tenure. I think that that era is coming to an end, and maybe the Constitutional Treaty will be the last great set-piece negotiation.

We now, as others before me have pointed out in this collection, profit from an environment in Brussels characterised by a far more positive attitude to economic liberalism than was previously the case. It is also an environment in which diversity is regarded as a fact of life, given the need to learn to operate at 25. This, too, is a development that suits the UK. One of my predecessors as Permanent Representative, and a fellow contributor to this collection, used to say—and he was absolutely right to do so—that 'the problem with this town is that there is too much religion and not enough politics'. I think that has changed a bit, for this is now a very political town. It is partly so because of the increasing prominence of the European Parliament. Partly, too, because a wave of legislation—largely Single Market related—has created a profound linkage between what happens in Brussels and the interests of a whole range of organisations and institutions in the private and public sector in every member state. The now EU matters to a variety of stakeholders across Europe and impinges directly on the substance of national public policy across virtually the whole range of policy sectors. The accumulation of legislation—particularly in the late 1980s and through the 1990s—means that the interrelationship between the domestic agenda and the Brussels agenda is greater now than it was five or ten years ago, and that tendency will continue to become more marked. And this, too, plays into the notion of Brussels being a more political town.

Because Brussels is now a very political town, people like me have to carry out the sorts of tasks to which Nigel Sheinwald has referred. We have to be prepared to get outside the formal negotiating process and think and act informally and politically. It is a good thing, because it moves us a little bit away from the ideological environment (too much religion and not enough politics) towards one which is more prosaic, more routinised and probably more UK-friendly.

Negotiation is still, of course, a core part of the Permanent Representative's role, but not perhaps in quite the same way it was ten years ago, and it is carried out in a different kind of environment. In my earlier incarnation as a member of UKRep I was responsible for negotiations in the area of external relations, which were very formal. When I now talk to colleagues who deal with the non-external policy agenda, their roles are far more varied.

© The Political Quarterly Publishing Co. Ltd. 2004

Thus they are, for instance, very conscious of the importance of the European Parliament. So negotiation for them is not simply about sitting in a working group, but also involves going down to Strasbourg and talking to MEPs about the development of legislation. Negotiations, therefore, have a broader scope—indeed almost by definition because of the accumulation of new functions for UKRep. UKRep is now much bigger than it used to be and either we are extremely inefficient or we are dealing with a broader range of activity. The staff of UKRep now number some 140—in comparison with 80 to 90 less than ten years ago.

Conclusions: coping with change

ANAND MENON

The foregoing discussions have provided a number of insights into the role of the Permanent Representative, the workings of the EC/EU system, and the relationship between Britain and the EC/EU. Without aspiring to an exhaustive discussion of all of them, this conclusion attempts to tease out the major issues touched upon by the various contributors.

The Permanent Representative in the British administrative system

The first clear conclusions that emerge relate to the nature of the post of Permanent Representative and the profiles of its various holders. There has been a marked tendency in recent years to appoint people who have had significant experience of EU affairs. Both Nigel Sheinwald and John Grant had worked in UKRep prior to taking the top job within it, as well as holding numerous other EU-related posts. Whilst Stephen Wall had no prior experience of working in UKRep, he had worked on EU matters and, crucially, given the political context at the time of his appointment to Brussels, had, via his experience as Private Secretary to Geoffrey Howe, Douglas Hurd and John Major, close personal relations with the most senior figures in the Conservative administration,

Prior expertise has been bolstered, moreover, by longevity, as John Kerr points out in his contribution. The fact that British Permanent Representatives tend to remain in post for longer than their counterparts from the other member states has, according to Kerr, tended to confer upon them a degree of authority that serves to enhance their influence within COREPER. And if that were not enough, the wide-ranging experience that appointees have had of EU affairs has generally been reinforced by the fact that, once in Brussels, they have tended to work closely with their predecessors and hence have been able to draw on the experience of the latter. This has been true since the earliest days, when Donald Maitland was waiting with the assembled press corps outside the room within which Michael Palliser was ensconced with Edward Heath and Georges Pompidou, to more recent times, when Nigel Sheinwald worked closely with all three of his predecessors.

Moreover, whilst none of the contributors, for obvious reasons, felt the need to mention it, the career trajectories of former ambassadors themselves provide clues as to the importance of the posting and the calibre of those who have held it. The two most recent Permanent Representatives were both appointed as advisers to Prime Minister Tony Blair, whilst, before them, John Kerr went on to head the Foreign and Commonwealth Office and David Hannay moved to the top position in the UK's representation to the UN. In other words, a post seen by all of its incumbents as one of the most interesting and intellectually stimulating of their careers is also often a stepping stone to still more prestigious appointments.

The Permanent Representative heads an organisation—UKRep—which is unlike any other British Embassy in that a large proportion of its staff hail from the Home Civil Service. Its numbers have, in recent years, been supplemented both by representatives of the devolved administrations and officials brought in to deal with newer policy areas, particularly the European Security and Defence Policy.[20] Several of the contributors underline the high calibre of the staff seconded to UKRep by both the Foreign Office and the home departments. Moreover, whilst occasional problems do occur as a result of the particular instructions received by one official from his or her home department, the impression given is that these are usually effectively resolved via the normal coordination processes.

Indeed, a striking feature of the foregoing contributions has been the emphasis placed on the close involvement of the Permanent Representative in the Whitehall–EU policy coordination process. John Kerr discusses at some length the importance of UKRep being 'embedded in Whitehall', of the Permanent Representative being immersed in the technical dossiers and in close contact with the relevant ministries in Whitehall. Formal participation in the coordination process occurs via the Permanent Representative's attendance at the Friday morning coordination meeting at the Cabinet Office, which brings together the Head of the European Secretariat of the Cabinet Office along with representatives of the Foreign and Commonwealth Office and of the major line ministries with an interest in ongoing discussions within the Union. Intuitively, there is good reason to suspect that this participation enhances the coordination capabilities of the UK system, as one of the few academic studies dealing directly with the role of Permanent Representations has argued:

the greater the involvement of the official from the permanent representation in the formulation of the national position, the easier it will be for him/her to negotiate in Brussels, in that they will have a clearer idea of the national problems and the margin of manoeuvre granted to them.[21]

Virtually all of the contributors stress the importance of effective coordination. Michael Butler learnt to his (and the country's) cost the problems that could be engendered by a failure to get Whitehall mobilised in a timely manner, on the occasion of the accession negotiations of 1962. The situation has changed beyond recognition in recent times, with Whitehall becoming more and more adept at dealing with Brussels. John Kerr singles out the example of the Home Office—a department which, prior to Maastricht, 'barely knew that the EC existed' but which was actively engaged in shaping the government's negotiating aims for the Convention on the Future of Europe.

Indeed, the overwhelming thrust of the contributions to this collection is hugely positive about the functioning of the system in place in the UK for the

40

coordination of EU policy. Yet it is possible that the picture is not as rosy as they imply, for at least two reasons. First, devolution. Nigel Sheinwald is characteristically upbeat about its impact on the coordination of EU policy in the UK, commenting that it has had the effect of strengthening the British system. Yet this assessment is surely contingent on political factors. The Scotland Act contains a potentially important tension, reserving specific policy areas—including the negotiation of European policy—to Westminster, whilst devolving several policy areas in which the EU is particularly active—notably agriculture, fisheries, environment, transport and regional policy. These policies 'revert' to the UK government when an EU legislative proposal or policy statement is under consideration. Consequently, there is a need for effective cooperative arrangements between the UK government and devolved administrations.[22] Whilst the evidence since devolution suggests that this has indeed been achieved, the question remains as to whether it will be possible to maintain such effective cooperation should the political complexions of the British government and the Scottish executive come to diverge—particularly given the different approaches to European integration adopted by the two major political parties.

The British system for the coordination of EU policy also raises broader questions relating to both the UK's policies and attitudes towards European integration, and the nature and effectiveness of the EU itself. In terms of the former, the United Kingdom has traditionally favoured an approach to coordination that stresses the need for coherence and tight centralisation. As Peter Pooley, an official formerly of the Ministry of Agriculture Food and Fisheries and UKRep, put it:

The British have an obsession with consistency which I think stems from the nature of our politics. Ministers must say the same as civil servants, civil servants the same as ministers . . . And so the British are more predictable. They are very well briefed, they are very articulate, it's very easy to get hold of and understand their point of view.[23]

He goes on, however, to point out that one of the side-effects of this approach is that it tends to limit the flexibility enjoyed by British negotiators. Thus, whilst effective coordination allows for the clear formulation of a national position, it may also serve to impede the quest for effectiveness at the EU level, where coalition building, particularly under QMV, is a necessity and where success depends on retaining enough bargaining chips to make it through to the endgame.

Crucially, the effectiveness of any given coordination strategy is dependent on the nature of the broader policy objectives espoused. Thus a tight, centralised system of coordination might well be the most appropriate way to pursue essentially defensive policy ambitions which stress the need to protect national interests, and to ensure that negative developments are prevented. Indeed, the arrangements put in place by the UK may be explained in terms of that very imperative.[24] It may not, however, be best suited to the pursuit of a more positive and proactive European strategy, in that the lack of negotiating flexibility engendered by a policy position that has emerged from a process of tight coordination does not militate in favour of compromise in Brussels. This problem was highlighted during recent negotiations over the draft constitutional treaty. On the one hand, Downing Street issued repeated calls for Whitehall to adopt a positive tone and proactive approach to the discussions. On the other, the inevitable upshot of the normal coordination procedures was that each line ministry had the opportunity to object to those parts of the document that impinged upon its own work, leading to a familiarly exhaustive list of British complaints, queries and amendments.[25]

Finally, the British style of coordination also has implications pertaining to the effectiveness of the Union itself. Successive British governments have found the coordination system in place in Whitehall to be a remarkably effective way of defending British policy positions in Brussels. Yet were other member states to put in place equally effective, centralised coordination mechanisms, this would seriously imperil the effectiveness of the Union and the ability of the Council to reach decisions. The relative inefficiency of coordination arrangements in several of the member states provides the necessary 'slack' that allows compromises to be reached in the Council. In other words, ineffective national coordination systems are arguably functional at the EU level. Emulation of the British system is not therefore something that London should encourage unless paralysis of the Council becomes a British policy objective.

A Union in flux

Perhaps unsurprisingly, the subject of the recent enlargement of the Union was one that came up frequently in the contributions of the more recent Permanent Representatives. One place where the impact of enlargement has already been keenly felt is within COREPER. The insights provided by the contributions of earlier Permanent Representatives certainly conform to the sociological perspective outlined by Jeffery Lewis and referred to in my introduction to this collection. Several of them point to the fact of COREPER being a club which operates in a good humoured way,[26] based on close personal relationships even at times of political tensions—such as during the British budgetary dispute. Indeed most of the contributors are at pains to emphasise that the various ambassadors see their roles in terms not only of getting the agreement they want, but also of helping their colleagues in COREPER do likewise. Michael Butler and John Kerr make the point that EU negotiations are not normally a zero-sum game.

More recent post holders point to a potentially significant shift in the organisational style of COREPER, linked to the expansion in its numbers. Whilst the club-like atmosphere of the committee was preserved in a Union of 12 member states, it would appear that this changed upon the EFTAn enlargement of 1995, which increased the membership of the Union to 15, and is changing still more dramatically in the wake of the most recent—and largest ever—enlargement. The committee has come more and more to

42

resemble a conference, despite moves to limit the size of each national delegation. Moreover, the utility of COREPER lunches, stressed by earlier Permanent Representatives as a useful tool for problem solving (Michael Butler mentions using one such occasion to come to a deal on terminology with his German counterpart, which proved crucial in the resolution of the British budgetary dispute) has diminished as sheer size necessitates the presence of microphones at these events. The loss of the intimacy that historically characterised COREPER looks likely to rob the Council of an instrument whose flexibility created a capacity for improvisation not found elsewhere within the Union's complex structures.

Changes in the composition and *modus operandi* of COREPER are one of a number of evolutions to which successive Permanent Representatives have had to adapt, and which have seen the nature of the job alter significantly. Another has been the growth in the power and influence of the European Parliament, partly as a function of the increased importance of the co-decision procedure, partly relative to what Stephen Wall refers to as the demise of the European Commission.[27] Whilst Permanent Representatives have always had to deal with Commission officials, and particularly with European Commissioners, more recent post holders have had to spend increasing amounts of time in Strasbourg, negotiating with and lobbying amongst MEPs who have come to wield an ever greater influence over legislative outcomes. This stands in stark contrast to earlier times, during which, as Michael Butler testifies, the Permanent Representative merely made a monthly trip to Strasbourg to brief British MEPs. Moreover, the active attempt to ensure that parliamentarians are informed of the national capital's thinking on key issues is a factor that distinguishes UKREP from many other permanent representations.[28]

Finally, as the scope of EU policies has expanded, and as their impact on policies within the member states has increased, more and more actors have begun to take an interest in 'Brussels'. Nigel Sheinwald points out that the increased mobilisation of interest groups has engendered a concomitant expansion in the scope of the tasks confronting Permanent Representatives, who now spend increasing amounts of time dealing with groups ranging from lobbyists to academics to NGOs. No longer does the post of Permanent Representative entail the heavy emphasis on negotiations within COREPER that it once did. The responsibilities of the post are now far more varied and extend far beyond the negotiation of technical dossiers to political lobbying and public diplomacy. As a consequence, a post that was already stressful and time consuming—witness Michael Butler's missed dinners with his wife, or John Kerr's snoring outside Harrods—has become, if anything, more so.

This bears eloquent testimony to the profound changes that have occurred in the nature of European integration, changes that are not captured by the rather blunt academic catchphrases associated with neofunctionalism or intergovernmentalism. Eschewing the scholarly infatuation with the question of sovereignty, the contributors have underlined that what has occurred is that the Union has become denser, more complex, or—in the words of John

Grant—more 'political'. The implications for the relative positions of the various member states remain, at best, unclear.

Enlargement, Euroscepticism and European integration

The various changes that have occurred and are underlined by the contributors have also had profound implications in terms of the nature of the relationship between the UK and the EU. On the one hand, several of the contributors are at pains to point out that the way in which the EC/EU has developed since the mid-1980s has been such as to benefit the UK. The increasingly widespread acceptance of economic liberalism, evidenced (ironically) by EMU and by the rise of the regulatory state at the EU level; the reduction in the amount of EU legislative activity (John Kerr speaks of the 'retreat from the notion that European integration is best built on ever wider EU powers and an ever bigger EU statute book'); the growth of lobbying activity, and hence of a more Anglo-Saxon policy style; the increasing predominance of English as the working language of the major institutions (more through good fortune, as Michael Palliser and John Kerr underline, than through any strategy on the part of British governments); as well as the greater acceptance of both the need for diversity in a Union of 25, and the legitimacy of accepting competition between systems, all seem to point in this direction. Moreover, recent enlargements have arguably reinforced the British position, notably with the accession of member states who share London's pro-American leanings (as Nigel Sheinwald stresses with his brief exposition of the maths of the Iraq crisis in the Council). Finally, whatever the hesitancies involved, the recent trend towards trilateral summits bringing together the British, French and Germans would seem to point to the fact that the UK has an opportunity to enhance its influence as Franco-German leadership proves inadequate for a Union of 25.[29]

Yet on the other hand, and paradoxically, as the Union has become more UK-friendly, the tone of political debate and media reporting within Britain has become more acerbic. The Murdoch, Black (as was) and Rothermere presses have become increasingly vitriolic in their hostility towards the European Union. Nigel Sheinwald has referred to the fact that the press in general has tended to prefer negative headlines of the 'UK isolated' type to more balanced reporting of long-term developments, such as enlargement (a point echoed by Michael Butler). Whilst one should, perhaps, remember with gratitude that a century ago, the headline would have been 'continent isolated', the tone adopted by the media has done little to fuel either understanding of what the EU is for or how it operates, or sympathy for the integration process (though, as John Kerr points out, the tone of the tabloid media can sometimes help Permanent Representatives in their efforts to persuade Commissioners to drop potentially highly unpopular initiatives). Politicians and their advisers, moreover, have been only too happy to foster such tendencies. Michael Butler points out that Bernard Ingham. Margaret Thatcher's spokesman, 'always wanted to make the European Council sound like a battlefield on which [Mrs Thatcher's] colleagues were routed'.

Media coverage has fed into an increasingly febrile political atmosphere surrounding the issue of European integration. Political constraints, as Stephen Wall reveals so clearly, have impacted profoundly on the nature of the policies pursued towards the Union by successive governments, and in far more direct and constraining ways than in the 1970s, when Michael Palliser and Geoffrey Ripon sat up late in the Council building counting the number of coastal Tory seats that would be affected by the Common Fisheries Policy.

The combination of a hostile media and criticism from both benches in the House of Commons has severely restricted the freedom of manoeuvre of British governments. As a consequence, the signals given by London in its EU policies have ranged from the confused to the downright hostile, irrespective of the undoubted talents of those charged with negotiating on behalf of British politicians. As Kassim and Peters put it, '[n]o matter how skilled the messenger, the message is what counts',[30] as David Hannay discovered at the time of Margaret Thatcher's Bruges speech of 1988. Whatever the strengths of the British administrative system, the fact that successive British governments have faced such venomous, if misplaced, criticism at home when it comes to dealing with the EU has increasingly tended to leave the country looking isolated and out of step with its partners—to the point where, as Stephen Wall comments, John Major's administration provoked Britain's partners to ask 'themselves whether it was possible for the British Government to sustain its commitment to the basic precepts of membership'.

Of course it may be, as alluded to above, that the latest enlargement will alter this situation by providing London with more natural allies. Certainly when, in December 2003, the talks over the constitutional treaty collapsed, it was refreshing to see that, for once, Britain was not isolated in the discussions. Yet the other side of the same coin is that not being isolated is hardly an impressive outcome for a government with a huge majority led by a genuinely pro-European Prime Minister who has repeatedly stated his intention to bring about, at the very least, some kind of 'normalisation' of relations between Britain (and the British) and the EU.[31]

More importantly, and more substantively, the problem confronting the British government is that pursuing the kind of EU that, as we have seen, increasingly favours British interests may require a willingness to address the Europhobes at home. David Hannay comments that Jacques Delors was never able to understand the hostility of the British towards the EC. And indeed, away from the headlines, the contributors have emphasised the close and productive relations that successive Permanent Representatives have enjoyed with officials from the European Commission. The Commission has, in fact, proved to be a staunch ally of successive British governments in the construction of a single market that, as the contributors have acknowledged, has suited British interests very well. At a time of rapid expansion, and when several member states are expressing disillusionment with the liberal workings of that market, that relationship remains as important as ever. Yet although Tony Blair acknowledged as much in an impressive (though under-reported) speech in Cardiff in November 2002,[32] it was not followed up by initiatives within the Convention or the Intergovernmental Conference, nor did it remain a recurrent theme of prime ministerial rhetoric.

On this reading, the government confronts a dilemma. It could adopt a more positive and proactive attitude towards the need for some reinforcement of the supranational institutions, in defiance of large sections of political and media opinion. Ideally, such an undertaking would be accompanied by an effort to be, in John Kerr's words, 'as positive and engaged in the domestic exposition of its EU policies as it is in their pursuit, so far rather successfully, in Brussels'. Alternatively, it could continue the approach of successive governments in running scared of the media and eurosceptics in parliament, and risk squandering the very benefits that Britain derives from the single market and that eurosceptics in this country have singularly failed to take into account.

Then again, perhaps this is too negative an outlook. The fact is that no one is really sure how the most recent enlargement will affect the workings of the Union, or Britain's place within it. It is possible that the influx of new members will lead to a strengthened and more liberal single market, even more to the liking of London than it currently is. What is clear, however, is that both the EU itself, and the nature of Britain's interactions and relationship with it, have altered profoundly over time and look likely to continue to do so in the future. At a minimum, it is to be hoped that this collection of essays will provoke thought about this complex and crucial subject.

Notes

1 J. W. de Zwann, *The Permanent Representatives Committee: Its Role in European Union Decision-Making*, Amsterdam, Elsevier, 1995, p. 25.
2 Ibid.; M. Westlake, *The Council of the European Union*, London, Cartermill International, 1995.
3 L. Barber, 'The men who run Europe', *Financial Times*, 11–12 March 1995.
4 For detailed discussions see V. Wright 'The national co-ordination of European policy-making: negotiating the quagmire', in J. Richardson (ed.), *The European Union: Policy and Power*, London, Routledge, 1997; H. Kassim, 'Introduction: Coordinating national action in Brussels', in H. Kassim, A. Menon, B. G. Peters and V. Wright (eds), *The National Co-ordination of EU Policy: The European Level*, Oxford, Oxford University Press, 2001.
5 A. Menon and V. Wright, 'The paradoxes of "failure": British EU policy making in comparative perspective', *Public Administration and Public Policy*, vol. 13, no. 4, 1998. See also H. Kassim 'The United Kingdom', in H. Kassim, B. G. Peters and V. Wright (eds), *The National Co-ordination of EU Policy Making: The Domestic Level*, Oxford, Oxford University Press, 2000.
6 H. Kassim, 'The United Kingdom'.
7 'COREPER' is the commonly used acronym derived from the French Comité des Représentants Permanents.
8 COREPER is in fact two separate institutions—COREPER I and COREPER II. The former is attended by the Deputy Permanent Representatives. The distribution of dossiers between the two is decided upon by the President of COREPER II—that is, by the Permanent Representative to the EU of the member state holding the Presidency of the Council. Whilst the precise remit of these committees has evolved over time, it is generally the case that COREPER I deals with more technical issues, whilst COREPER II handles the more sensitive Council formations.
9 Westlake, *The Council of the European Union*, p. 285.
10 See de Zwann, *The Permanent Representatives Committee*, pp. 25–70; Westlake, ibid., pp. 285–307, F. Hayes-Renshaw and H. Wallace, *The Council of Ministers*, Basingstoke, Macmillan, 1997, pp. 72–84.
11 J. Lewis, 'The Methods of Community in EU decision-making and administrative rivalry in the Council's infrastructure', *Journal of European Public Policy*, vol. 7, no. 2, June 2000, p. 263.
12 H. Kassim 'Introduction: Coordinating National Action in Brussels', p. 24.
13 L. Barber, 'The men who run Europe'. Note Helen Wallace's comment that '[n]ot only do the Representations represent and bargain on behalf of their governments but they have also become part of the Community system itself', *National Governments and the European Communities*, London, Chatham House and PEP, 1973, p. 56.
14 Lewis, 'The Methods of Community in EU decision-making', p. 266.
15 Ibid., p. 261.
16 S. George, *An Awkward Partner: Britain in the European Community*, Oxford, Oxford University Press, 1998.
17 Hugo Young, *This Blessed Plot: Britain and Europe from Churchill to Blair*, London, Macmillan, 1998.
18 [Editor's note] To put this into context, it should be remembered that amongst Sir John's other postings were stints as Ambassador in Washington, Permanent Under-

Secretary in the Foreign Commonwealth Office, and Secretary General of the Convention on the Future of Europe.

19 Hugo Young, *This Blessed Plot*.

20 According to John Grant in his contribution to this collection, the staff of UKRep now numbers some 140—in comparison with 80 to 90 less than 10 years ago.

21 Fiona Hayes-Renshaw, Christian Lequesne and Pedro Mayor Lopez, 'The permanent representations of the Member States to the European Communities', *Journal of Common Market Studies*, vol. 28, no. 2, December 1989, p. 130.

22 P. Hogwood, C. Carter, S. Bulmer, M. Burch and A. Scott, 'Devolution and EU policy making: the territorial challenge', *Public Policy and Administration*, vol. 15, no. 2, 2000, pp. 85–6.

23 Cited in G. Edwards, 'Central government', in S. George (ed.), *Britain and the European Community: The Politics of Semi-Detachment*, Oxford, Clarendon Press, 1992, p. 74.

24 For a discussion of this point see H. Derlien, 'Germany: failing successfully', in H. Kassim et al. (eds), *The National Co-ordination of EU Policy: The Domestic Level*.

25 See A. Menon, 'Leading from behind: Britain and the EU's constitutional treaty', *Notre Europe*, January 2004, available at: http://www.notre-europe.asso.fr/

26 One Permanent Representative informed me that, during a discussion of the disappointing outcome of the Amsterdam IGC, his French colleague had turned to the German representative and castigated him for representing a country in which the Lander exercised so much power over Federal Government negotiators. To which the latter responded, to general hilarity, that it had been the French who had insisted on the creation of a weakened, decentralised Germany in the first place (Interview, Brussels, 2000).

27 In the question and answer session that followed the presentations by the Ambassadors, Neil Kinnock reinforced this point, referring to the 'significant impact made on the whole context of conduct and diplomacy [within the EU] by the development of the European Parliament'.

28 See H. Kassim and B. G. Peters, 'Conclusion: Co-ordinating national action in Brussels—a comparative perspective' in H. Kassim et al. (eds), *The National Co-ordination of EU Policy: The European Level*.

29 For a discussion of recent attempts by the three to exercise leadership over the European Security and Defence Policy (ESDP), see A. Menon, 'From crisis to catharsis: ESDP after Iraq', *International Affairs*, July 2004.

30 Kassim and Peters, 'Conclusion: Co-ordinating national action in Brussels—a comparative perspective', p. 331.

31 Though see R. Denman, 'Blair's missed chance', *Prospect*, May 1998.

32 Tony Blair, 'A clear course for Europe', Cardiff, 28 November 2002, available at http://www.number-10.gov.uk/output/Page1739.asp

The Contributors

Anand Menon is Director of the European Research Institute and Professor of European Politics at the University of Birmingham.

Sir Michael Butler GCMG was Ambassador and UK Permanent Representative to the European Communities, Brussels, from 1979 to 1985.

Sir Michael was involved with EC affairs in Paris (1961–1965), Geneva (1968–1970) and Washington (1971–1972). He became Head of the European Integration Department of the FCO in June 1970, and was promoted to Assistant Under-Secretary in January 1974, just in time to assume responsibility for the so-called renegotiation of the terms of entry when Labour was elected at the end of February. He advised Mr Callaghan up to the successful conclusion of the negotiations in March 1975 and during the subsequent referendum. In 1976 he was appointed Deputy Secretary in charge of economic affairs, and advised Mr Crosland and Mr Owen until Mrs Thatcher won the 1979 election. Shortly afterwards he was posted to Brussels.

In 1985 he took early retirement and in 1986 published his guide to the EC, *Europe: More Than a Continent*. As an investment banker, he became Chairman of the City's European Committee (1988–1993) which originated the 'hard ecu' plan. He has been involved in EU affairs in many ways since then—as Labour's Ambassador to the Pre-Accession countries and adviser to Mr Robin Cook as Foreign Secretary (1996–1998). At present he is a member of the board of Britain in Europe and Chairman of its Senior Experts Committee.

John Grant CMG has been Ambassador and UK Permanent Representative to the European Communities, Brussels, since 2003.

John was born in Singapore in 1954 and educated at the Edinburgh Academy and St Catharine's College, Cambridge. He joined the Diplomatic Service in 1976, and served in Stockholm and Moscow before returning to London in 1984.

A year later he resigned and started work with Morgan Grenfell as part of a team dealing with the Soviet Union and Eastern Europe. Stimulating though this venture was, he decided that his future lay as a diplomat and he returned to the Foreign Office in 1986. This was followed by five years of press work, first in the News Department in London (for three years) and then in the UK Permanent Representation in Brussels.

After two years as UK spokesman in Brussels there followed six more years on EU issues until 1997 (all but six months of which were in Brussels), working on issues such as EU enlargement and the development of the EU's common foreign and security policy.

In 1997 he was appointed Principal Private Secretary to the Foreign Secretary, Robin Cook, and in 1999 was appointed to Stockholm as Ambassador.

Lord Hannay of Chiswick GCMG was Ambassador and UK Permanent Representative to the European Communities, Brussels, from 1985 to 1990.

Sir David Hannay was a British diplomat for thirty-six years, serving in Tehran, Kabul, Brussels (several times), Washington and New York. He was a member of the UK negotiating team for accession to the European Communities, and spent four years on secondment to the European Commission as Chef de Cabinet to Sir Christopher Soames, Vice President. He became Britain's Permanent Representative to the United Nations in 1990 and served until 1995.

Following his retirement from the Diplomatic Service in 1995 he was appointed British Special Representative for Cyprus, a post he held for seven years. Since 2001 he has been an Independent member of the House of Lords, where he is a member of the European Union Select Committee. He is currently serving as a member of the United Nations Secretary-General's High-Level Panel on Threats, Challenges and Change, and is Pro-Chancellor of the University of Birmingham.

Sir John Kerr GCMG was Ambassador and UK Permanent Representative to the European Communities, Brussels, from 1990 to 1995.

Born in Grantown-on-Spey and educated at Glasgow Academy, Sir John was a member of the UK Diplomatic Service from 1966 to 2002. After postings in Moscow, Islamabad, Washington, the Foreign Office and the Treasury (where he was Private Secretary to the Chancellor), he became the first UK diplomat to hold the Service's three top jobs: successively Permanent Representative to the EU, Ambassador to the United States, and FCO Permanent Under-Secretary.

As Ambassador to the European Communities, Sir John was, in 1991, the UK negotiator in the Monetary Union and Political Union IGCs. As Secretary General of the European Convention, he worked with President Giscard d'Estaing on the draft EU Constitutional Treaty.

Sir Donald Maitland GCMG OBE was Ambassador and UK Permanent Representative to the European Communities, Brussels, from 1975 to 1979.

Born in Edinburgh, Sir Donald was educated at George Watson's College and Edinburgh University. After wartime service in the Middle East, India and Burma, he joined the Foreign Service in 1947.

Sir Donald served in various posts in the Foreign Office and several in the Middle East. Between 1956 and 1960 he was Director of the Middle East Centre for Arab Studies in Lebanon. In 1967 he became Principal Private Secretary to the Foreign Secretary and later Ambassador to Libya. In the early 1970s he was appointed Chief Press Secretary to the Prime Minister. Sir Donald received his Knighthood in 1973. In the 1970s Sir Donald was the United Kingdom Permanent Representative to the United Nations in New York before moving to Brussels in 1975.

In 1980 Sir Donald became Permanent Under-Secretary of the Department of State for Energy. Later he became very involved in the development of world telecommunications, and was Chairman of the Independent Commission for World Wide Telecommunications Development from 1982 to 1985. In the late 1980s he was Deputy Chairman of the Independent Broadcasting Authority.

Sir Donald was Chairman of Governors of Westminster College, Oxford, between 1994 and 1997, and has been Pro-Chancellor of the University of Bath since 1996. He is also President of the Bath Institute for Rheumatic Diseases. In

November 2003 he was awarded an honorary Doctor of Letters by the University of the West of England in recognition of his outstanding contribution to the understanding of European international affairs, and is also currently a Visiting Professor at the University of Bath.

Rt Hon Sir Michael Palliser GCMG was Ambassador and UK Permanent Representative to the European Communities, Brussels, from 1973 to 1975.

Born in 1922 in Reigate, Surrey, Sir Michael was formerly the Permanent Under-Secretary of State, Foreign and Commonwealth Office. He entered the Diplomatic Service in 1947 after wartime service in the Coldstream Guards from 1942 to 1946, during which he was mentioned in despatches.

Sir Michael's foreign appointments have included Athens, Paris and Dakar. He progressed rapidly from Head of Planning Staff in the Foreign Office from 1964, to a Private Secretary to the Prime Minister from 1966 to 1969. He then became a minister in Paris from 1969 to 1970, followed by Ambassador and Head of the UK Delegation to the EEC between 1971 and 1972, and from 1975 to 1983 he served as the Permanent Under-Secretary, Head of Diplomatic Service.

Sir Michael is currently the Chair of the Council of the International Institute for Strategic Studies, a position he took up in 1983, and has been a director of many companies. In 1982 he was appointed an Associate Fellow of the Center for International Affairs at Harvard University, and from 1983 has been involved with the David Davies Memorial institute of International Studies. He is a Chevalier of the Order of Orange-Nassau, and of the Légion d'honneur.

Sir Nigel Sheinwald KCMG was Ambassador and UK Permanent Representative to the European Communities, Brussels, from 2000 to 2003.

Sir Nigel was born in 1953 and educated at Harrow County Grammar School and Balliol College, Oxford. He joined the Diplomatic Service in 1976 and has served in Brussels (twice), Washington and Moscow, and in a wide range of policy jobs in London. He took up his appointment as Foreign Policy Adviser to the Prime Minister in August 2003.

He served in Moscow (1978–1979) and was Head of the FCO Anglo-Soviet Section (1981–1983). Between 1983 and 1987 he worked in the Political Section of the British Embassy in Washington. From 1987 to 1989 he was Deputy Head of the FCO's Policy Planning Staff, responsible for transatlantic relations and other issues. Nigel Sheinwald has also worked on Japan (1976–1977) and Zimbabwe (1979–1981), including the Lancaster House Conference.

He was FCO Press Secretary and Head of News Department from 1995 to 1998. Prior to becoming UK Ambassador to the European Union in 2000, he was Europe Director in the FCO (1998–2000). He was Head of the UK Representation's Political and Institutional Section in Brussels in 1993–1995 and Deputy Head of the FCO's European Union (Internal) Department from 1989 to 1992. He was knighted in 2001.

Sir Stephen Wall KCMG was Ambassador and UK Permanent Representative to the European Communities, Brussels, from 1995 to 2000.

Sir Stephen was educated at Douai School and Selwyn College, Cambridge, and as well as serving as UK Permanent Representative to the EU he has served as the UK's Ambassador to Portugal. He was Private Secretary to David Owen and Peter Carrington before serving in Washington (1979–1983) as First Secretary responsible for reporting on US domestic politics and for dealing with Northern Ireland issues.

On return to London he was Assistant Head and then Head of the European Communities Department, dealing with the negotiations on the European Single Act. He subsequently worked as Private Secretary to three successive foreign secretaries (Geoffrey Howe, John Major and Douglas Hurd) and then as Private Secretary to John Major when the latter was Prime Minister.

From 2000 to mid-2004, Stephen was responsible for coordinating official advice on EU issues to the Prime Minister and other ministers, and was the Prime Minister's EU adviser in 10 Downing Street.

Stephen Wall left the Civil Service in June 2004 to become Principal Adviser to the Roman Catholic Archbishop of Westminster, Cardinal Cormac Murphy O'Connor.